Hymns and Meditations

by Miss A. L. Waring
This Edition Edited by Anthony Uyl

Devoted Publishing

Woodstock, Ontario, Canada 2018

Hymns and Meditations
by Miss A. L. Waring
with An Introduction by the RT. Rev. F. D. Huntington, D. D.
Bishop of Central New York
This Edition Edited by Anthony Uyl

What kind of philosophies do you have?
Let us know!

Visit our online store: www.devotedpublishing.com
Contact us at: devotedpub@hotmail.com
Visit us on Facebook: @DevotedPublishing

Published in Woodstock, Ontario, Canada 2018

For bulk educational rates, please contact us at the above email address.

ISBN: 978-1-77356-264-3

Table of Contents

INTRODUCTION.........................4

HYMN 1.....................................6

HYMN 2.....................................8

HYMN 3.....................................9

HYMN 4...................................10

HYMN 5...................................11

HYMN 6...................................12

HYMN 7...................................13

HYMN 8...................................14

HYMN 9...................................15

HYMN 10.................................16

HYMN 11.................................17

HYMN 12.................................18

HYMN 13.................................19

HYMN 14.................................20

HYMN 15.................................21

HYMN 16.................................23

HYMN 17.................................25

HYMN 18.................................28

HYMN 19.................................29

HYMN 20.................................30

HYMN 21.................................33

HYMN 22.................................36

HYMN 23.................................39

HYMN 24.................................40

HYMN 25.................................42

HYMN 26.................................44

HYMN 27.................................46

HYMN 28.................................49

HYMN 29.................................50

HYMN 30.................................52

HYMN 31.................................54

HYMN 32.................................56

INTRODUCTION

The reasons that induce me to recommend the republication of this little volume are easily stated. It belongs to a class of devotional writings having a peculiar ministry and a peculiar value, -- a value not the less real because it is not the fashion of the age to magnify it. The class is not large; but within it this work takes a high place. The tone of spiritual thought and feeling in most of the pieces is very lofty and very pure. The ideas of a Christian life which are wrought into the poetry are always both strong and tender, vigorous and gentle, brave and trustful. We find few traces of that refined religious selfishness on the one hand, and that feeble sentimentalism on the other, which vitiate so much of the pious literature, and especially the metrical pious literature, of modern times. A state of comfortable pietistic complacency is not here put instead of a self-renouncing submission to the perfect will of God, nor does the call to action ring out with the less clearness and power, because we see laid open before us the divine depths of a complete and serene communion with the indwelling Christ. It is not common to meet with the expression of a more profound, more healthy, more childlike faith, or in more chaste, beautiful, and harmonious words, than in the lyrics numbered 8, 14, 15, 17, 19, 20, 25, 26, and 32. These alone would justify the claims of a book taking much more room than this one.

Undoubtedly, there are degrees in the poetical merit of the different pieces in the volume, as might be expected. It would be unreasonable to imply that these unpretending songs are, in whole or in part, proofs of the possession of the very loftiest degree of the creative gift, or to presume that all Christian minds will prize them equally. But tastes are so various, that it is safe to include all that appear in the London edition. Indeed, there is hardly one that does not bear upon it at least some slight trace of a refined perception and a select faculty; as, for example: --

"And let my moments, as they flee,
*Unfold my endless life in Thee!"**

*"A heart at leisure from itself"**

*"Songs of defence my soul surround."**

"On thee my humbled soul would wait,
*Her utmost weakness calmly learning."**

"A life of self-renouncing love
*Is a life of liberty."**

"Put doubts of my affection by,
And make me free to sing of thine."*

"For all the work I have to do,
Is done through strengthening rest in thee."*

"And when Thy joy the Church o'erflows,
I know that it will visit me."*

Into such stanzas as the following inventive thought and holy trust crowd their meaning compactly and yet musically --

"Oft in a dark and lonely place,
I hush my hastened breath,
To hear the comfortable words
Thy loving Spirit saith;
And feel my safety in thy hand
From every kind of death."*

"Glory to thee for strength withheld,
For want and weakness known, --
The fear that sends me to thy breast
For what is most my own.
I have a heritage of joy
That yet I must not see;
The hand that bled to make it mine
Is keeping it for me."*

"Henceforth, whate'er my heart's desire,
Fulfil in me thy own design;
I need the Fountain and the Fire,
And both, O King of saints, are thine."*

Nor will any reader who has ever made a study of style fail to notice the frequent occurrence of fine discriminations in the application of terms, of delicate shades of imaginative coloring, and of a certain reserve and self-command in the use of fancy when there was an obvious temptation to a much more prodigal expenditure of it. Repeatedly we find line after line of words of a single syllable. Such simplicity is not often found except in union with strength. One is led to believe that this is one of those instances where intellectual originality is both developed and disciplined by the energy of a spiritual life in the soul. It is doubtful whether the author would ever have appeared as a genius, if "the eyes of her understanding" had not been "enlightened" by that "love of Christ which passeth knowledge;" -- so comprehending "what is the length and breadth and depth and height."

F. D. H.
BOSTON, Day of the Annunciation, 1863

HYMN 1

"My times are in Thy hand." -- Psalm 31:15

Father, I know that all my life
Is portioned out for me,
And the changes that are sure to come,
I do not fear to see;
But I ask Thee for a present mind
Intent on pleasing Thee.

I ask Thee for a thoughtful love,
Through constant watching wise,
To meet the glad with joyful smiles,
And to wipe the weeping eyes;
And a heart at leisure from itself,
To soothe and sympathize.

I would not have the restless will
That hurries to and fro,
Seeking for some great thing to do,
Or secret thing to know;
I would be treated as a child,
And guided where I go.

Wherever in the world I am,
In whatsoe'er estate,
I have a fellowship with hearts
To keep and cultivate;
And a work of lowly love to do
For the Lord on whom I wait.

So I ask Thee for the daily strength,
To none that ask denied,
And a mind to blend with outward life
While keeping at Thy side;
Content to fill a little space,
If Thou be glorified.

And if some things I do not ask,
In my cup of blessing be,
I would have my spirit filled the more
With grateful love to Thee --
More careful -- not to serve Thee much,
But to please Thee perfectly.

There are briers besetting every path,
That call for patient care;
There is a cross in every lot,
And an earnest need for prayer;
But a lowly heart that leans on Thee
Is happy anywhere.

In a service which Thy will appoints,
There are no bonds for me;
For my inmost heart is taught "the truth"
That makes Thy children "free;"
And a life of self-renouncing love,
Is a life of liberty.

HYMN 2

"Thou maintainest my lot." -- Psalm 16:5.

Source of my life's refreshing springs,
Whose presence in my heart sustains me,
Thy love appoints me pleasant things,
Thy mercy orders all that pains me.

If loving hearts were never lonely,
If all they wish might always be,
Accepting what they look for only,
They might be glad, but not in Thee.

Well may Thy own beloved, who see
In all their lot their Father's pleasure,
Bear loss of all they love, save Thee,
Their living, everlasting treasure.

Well may Thy happy children cease
From restless wishes prone to sin,
And, in Thy own exceeding peace,
Yield to Thy daily discipline.

We need as mnch the cross we bear,
As air we breathe, -- as light we see;
It draws us to Thy side in prayer,
It binds us to our strength in Thee.

HYMN 3

"If ye shall ask anything in my name, I will do it." -- John 14:14.

My prayer to the promise shall cling --
I will not give heed to a doubt;
For I ask for the one needful thing,
Which I cannot be happy without.

A spirit of lowly repose
In the love of the Lamb that was slain,
A heart to be touched with his woes,
And a care not to grieve Him again --

The peace that my Savior has bought,
The cheerfulness nothing can dim,
The love that can bring every thought
Into perfect obedience to Him --

The wisdom his mercy to own
In the way he directs me to take, --
To glory in Jesus alone,
And to love, and do good for His sake.

All this Thou hast offered to me
In the promise whereon I will rest;
For faith, O my Savior, in Thee,
Is the substance of all my reqnest.

Thy word has commanded my prayer,
Thy Spirit has taught me to pray;
And all my unholy despair
Is ready to vanish away.

Thou wilt not be weary of me,
Thy promise my faith will sustain,
And soon, very soon, I shall see
That I have not been asking in vain.

HYMN 4

"I, even I, am He that comforteth you." -- Isaiah 2:12

Sweet is the solace of Thy love,
My Heavenly Friend, to me,
While through the hidden way of faith
I journey home with Thee,
Learning by quiet thankfulness
As a dear child to be.

Though from the shadow of Thy peace
My feet would often stray,
Thy mercy follows all my steps,
And will not turn away;
Yea, thou wilt comfort me at last,
As none beneath Thee may.

Oft in a dark and lonely place,
I hush my hastened breath,
To hear the comfortable words
Thy loving Spirit saith;
And feel my safety in Thy hand
From every kind of death.

O there is nothing in the world
To weigh against Thy will;
Even the dark times I dread the most
Thy covenant filfil;
And when the pleasant morning dawns
I find Thee with me still.

Then in the secret of my soul,
Though hosts my peace invade,
Though through a waste and weary land
My lonely way he made,
Thou, even Thou, wilt comfort me --
I need not be afraid.

Still in the solitary place
I would awhile abide,
Till with the solace of Thy love
My heart is satisfied;
And all my hopes of happiness
Stay calmly at Thy side.

HYMN 5

"I will pour water on him that is thirsty, and floods upon the dry ground."
-- Isaiah 44:8.

Source of my spirit's deep desire
For living joys that shall not perish,
The patient hope Thy words inspire,
Still let Thy tender mercy cherish.

On Thee my humbled soul would wait,
Her utmost weakness calmly learning,
And see Thy grace its way create,
Through thorns and briers which Thou art burning.

Gladly my inmost heart would know
The love that now it faintly traces,
And see the streams from Zion flow
O'er all its waste and desert places.

And still I hope -- O not in vain!
I know, this ho]y seed possessing,
Thou wilt come down like gentle rain,
And make the barren ground a blessing.

HYMN 6

"The Lord blessed the Seventh day and hallowed it." -- Exodus 20:11.

Beam on us brightly, blessed day,
Dawn softly for our Savior's sake;
And waft thy sweetness o'er our way,
To draw us heavenward when we wake.

O holy life that shall not end,
Light that will never cease to be --
May every Sabbath-day we spend,
Add to our happiness in Thee.

HYMN 7

"In returning and rest shall ye be saved; in quietness and confidence shall be your strength." -- Isaiah 30:15.

With a heart full of anxious request,
Which my Father in heaven bestowed,
I wandered alone, and distressed,
In search of a quiet abode.
Astray and distracted I cried, --
Lord, where would'st Thou have me to be?
And the voice of the Lamb that had died
Said, Come, my beloved, to ME.

I went -- for He mightily wins
Weary souls to His peaceful retreat --
And He gave me forgiveness of sins,
And songs that I love to repeat;
And oft as my enemies came,
My views of His glory to dim,
He taught me to trust in His name,
And to triumph by leaning on Him.

Made pure by the blood that He shed,
My heart in His presence was free;
I was hungry and thirsty -- He fed;
I was sick, and he comforted me;
He gave me the blessing complete --
The hope that is with me today,
And a quiet abode at his feet,
That shall not be taken away.

HYMN 8

"The Lord is the portion of mine inheritance." -- Psalm 16:5.

Though some good things of lower worth
My heart is called on to resign,
Of all the gifts in heaven and earth,
The greatest and the best is mine
The love of God in Christ made known --
The love that is enough alone,
My Father's love is all my own.

My soul's Restorer, let me learn
In that deep love to live and rest --
Let me the precious thing discern
Of which I am indeed possessed.
My treasure let me feel and see,
And let my moments, as they flee,
Unfold my endless life in Thee.

Let me not dwell so much within
My bounded heart, with anxious heed --
Where all my searches meet with sin,
And nothing satisfies my need --
It shuts me from the sound and sight
Of that pure world of life and light,
Which has no breadth, or length, or height.

Let me Thy power, Thy beauty see;
So shall the hopeless labor cease,
And my free heart shall follow thee
Through paths of everlasting peace.
My strength Thy gift, -- my life Thy care, --
I shall forget to seek elsewhere
The wealth to which my soul is heir.

I was not called to walk alone,
To clothe myself with love and light;
And for Thy glory, not my own,
My soul is precious in Thy sight.
My evil heart can never be
A home, a heritage for me --
But Thou canst make it fit for Thee.

HYMN 9

"I will fear no evil, for thou art with me." -- Psalm 23:4.

In Heavenly Love abiding,
No change my heart shall fear,
And safe is such confiding,
For nothing changes here.
The storm may roar without me,
My heart may low be laid,
Bnt God is round about me,
And can I be dismayed?

Wherever He may guide me,
No want shall turn me back;
My Shepherd is beside me,
And nothing can I lack.
His wisdom ever waketh,
His sight is never dim, --
He knows the way He taketh,
And I will walk with Him.

Green pastures are before me,
Which yet I have not seen;
Bright skies will soon be o'er me,
Where the dark clouds have been.
My hope I cannot measure,
My path to life is free,
My Savior has my treasure,
And He will walk with me.

HYMN 10

"There is a friend that sticketh closer than a brother." -- Proverbs 18:24.

Would that I were more closely bound
To my Beloved, who ever lives;
Would that my soul were always found
Abiding in the peace He gives;
Would, that I might more clearly see
His love an heritage for me
More surely know, more meekly own,
His bounteous grace my strength alone!

And much I wish but I will pray
For wisdom that the lowly find, --
And, O my Savior, every day,
More of Thy meek and quiet mind.
The comfort of a mind at rest
From every care Thou hast not blest,
A heart from all the world set free,
To worship and to wait on Thee.

Ah! my Beloved who wilt not die,
Whose spirit does not change with mine,
Put doubts of my affection by,
And make me free to sing of Thine.
The more Thy goodness I confess,
I shall not surely love Thee less;
The more myself alone I see,
The farther off I feel from Thee.

Thou art my life's restoring rest,
In Thee for safety let me hide, --
And win me for Thy grateful guest
By love that will not be denied.
Try me with Thy refining fire,
Array me in Thy white attire,
Be Wisdom, Righteousness to me,
The River of my pleasures be,
And fill my life with love of Thee.

HYMN 11

"I will bless the Lord at all times." -- Psalm 34:1.

Tender mercies, on my way
Falling softly like the dew,
Sent me freshly every day,
I will bless THE LORD for you.

Though I have not all I would,
Though to greater bliss I go,
Every present gift of good
To Eternal Love I owe.

Source of all that comforts me,
Well of joy for which I long,
Let the song I sing to Thee
Be an everlasting song.

HYMN 12

"Thou, Lord, art good, and ready to forgive; and plenteous in mercy unto all them that call upon Thee." -- Psalm 86:5.

My Savior whose infinite grace
Most kindly encompasses me,
Whose goodness more brightly I trace,
The more of my life that I see. --
The sins that I mournfully own,
Thy meekness and mercy exalt, --
And sweet is the voice from Thy throne,
That tenderly shows me a fault.

Even now, while my praises arise,
A sorrowful spirit is mine;
A spirit Thou wilt not despise,
For O! it is mourning with Thine.
My joy is in light from above,
The light which Thy kindness displays;
My grief is for lack of the love
That would tune my whole life to Thy praise.

My faithful Redeemer, forgive
The sin it has grieved Thee to see,
And let me remember to live
In the Spirit that glorifies Thee.
Though much in Thy child Thou hast borne,
Thy counsels still gently repeat,
And give me, if still I must mourn,
To mourn as a child at thy feet.

HYMN 13

"I will trust in the covert of Thy wings." -- Psalm 61:4.

Under Thy wings, my God, I rest
Under Thy shadow safely lie;
By Thy own strength in peace possessed,
While dreaded evils pass me by.

With strong desire I here can stay
To see Thy love its work complete;
Here I can wait a long delay,
Reposing at my Savior's feet.

My place of lowly service, too,
Beneath Thy sheltering wings I see;
For all the work I have to do
Is done through strengthening rest in Thee.

I would not rise this rest above;
I do not mourn my low estate
Sure of my riches in Thy love,
I feel it good to trust and wait.

In faith and patience is repose;
In faith and rest my strength shall be;
And when thy joy the church o'erflows,
I know that it will visit me.

HYMN 14

"For the Lord shall comfort Zion; He will comfort all her waste places; and He will make her wilderness like Eden, and her desert like the garden of the Lord; joy and gladness shall be found therein, thanksgiving, and the voice of melody."
-- Isaiah 51:3.

"Sing, O Heavens; and be joyful, O Earth; for the Lord hath comforted his people." -- Isaiah 49:13.

A living, loving, lasting word,
My listening ear believing heard,
While bending down in prayer;
Like a sweet breeze that none can stay,
It passed my soul upon its way,
And left a blessing there.

Then joyful thoughts that come and go,
By paths the holy angels know,
Encamped around my soul;
As in a dream of blest repose,
Mid withered reeds a river rose,
And through the desert stole.

I lifted up my eyes to see --
The wilderness was glad for me,
Its thorns were bright with bloom;
And onward travellers still in sight,
Marked out a path of shining light,
And shade unmixed with gloom.

O sweet the strains of those before,
"The weary knees are weak no more,
The faithful heart is strong;"
But sweeter, nearer, from above,
That word of everlasting love,
The promise and the song.

HYMN 15

"I wait for the Lord, my soul doth wait, and in His word do I hope."
-- Psalm 130:5.

My Savior, on the word of truth
In earnest hope I live;
I ask for all the precious things
Thy boundless love can give.
I look for many a lesser light
About my path to shine;
But chiefly long to walk with Thee,
And only trust in Thine.

In holy expectation held,
Thy strength my heart shall stay,
For Thy right hand will never let
My trust be cast away.
Yea, Thou hast kept me near Thy feet,
In many a deadly strife,
By the stronghold of hope in Thee,
The hope of endless life.

Thou knowest that I am not blest
As Thou wouldst have me be,
Till all the peace and joy of faith
Possess my soul in Thee
And still I seek 'mid many fears,
With yearnings unexpressed,
The comforts of Thy strengthening love,
Thy soothing, settling rest.

It is not as Thou wilt with me,
Till, humbled in the dust;
I know no place in all my heart
Wherein to put my trust.
Until I find, O Lord, in Thee,
The Lowly and the Meek,
That fulness which Thy own redeemed
Go nowhere else to seek.

Then, O my Savior, on my soul,
Cast down, but not dismayed,
Still be Thy chastening, healing hand
In tender, mercy laid.

And while I wait for all Thy joys,
My yearning heart to fill,
Teach me to walk and work with Thee,
And at Thy feet sit still.

HYMN 16

A NEW YEAR'S MORNING SONG.
"He hath put a new song in my mouth, even thanksgiving unto our God."
-- Psalm 40:3.

Thanksgiving and the voice of melody,
This new year's morning, call me from my sleep;
A new, sweet song is in my heart for Thee,
Thou faithful, tender Shepherd of the sheep;
Thou knowest where to find, and how to keep
The feeble feet that tremble where they stray, --
O'er the dark mountains -- through the whelming deep --
Thy everlasting mercy makes its way.

The past is not so dark as once it seemed,
For there Thy footprints, now distinct, I see;
And seed in weakness sown, from death redeemed,
Is springing up, and bearing fruit in Thee.
Not all that hath been, Lord, henceforth shall be;
A low, sweet, cheering strain is in mine ear,
Thanksgiving, and the voice of melody,
Are leading in, from Heaven, a blest new year.

With voice subdued, my listening spirit sings,
As backward on the trodden path I gaze,
While ministering angels fold their wings,
To fill with lowly thoughts my song of praise.
The shadow of the past on future days,
Will make them clear to my instructed sight;
For the heart's knowledge of Thy sacred ways,
Even in its deepest, darkest shades, is light.

I am not stronger -- yet I do not fear
The present pain, the conflict yet to be;
Experience is a kind voice in mine ear,
And all my failures bid me lean on Thee.
No future suffering can seem strange to me,
While in the hidden part I feel and know
The wisdom of a child at rest and free
In the tried love, whose judgment keeps him low.

Thanksgiving and the voice of melody!
O, to my tranquil heart how sweet the strain!
Father of mercies, it arose in Thee,

23

And to Thy bosom it returns again.
There let my grateful song, my soul, remain,
Calm in the risen Savior's tender care;
And welcome any trial, any pain,
That serves to keep thy faithful children there.

Thoughts of Thy love -- and O, how great the sum!
Enduring grief, obtaining bliss for me;
The world, life, death, things present, things to come,
All swell a new year's opening melody.
Past, present, future, all things worship Thee;
And I, through all, with trembling joy behold,
While mountains fall, and treacherous visions flee,
Thy wandering sheep returning to the fold.

HYMN 17

"Thou hast turned for me my mourning into dancing: Thou hast put off my sackcloth and girded me with gladness. To the end that my glory may sing praise to Thee, and not be silent. O Lord my God, I will give thanks unto Thee for ever." -- Psalm 30:11,12.

Strength of the still secluded thought,
That fears, yet longs its joy to show, --
The hope, the awe, in mercy taught
To make me strong, to keep me low;
Now shall my girded heart rejoice,
In praise poured out, in love expressed;
Now will I bless Thee, with a voice
That shall not break this sacred rest.

Once, moved by every mortal pain,
By every pleasure quickly past,
I feared to speak in joyful strain
Of hidden life that might not last.
Now, from a well that will not fail,
In Thee my deep rejoicing springs --
Now from Thy rest within the veil,
My spirit looks on passing things.

Once, with Thy tired ones homeward bent,
In hope that rose their fears above,
My leaping heart could be content
To greet them with a silent love;
I too had walked with weary feet,
And heard the exulting shout too near --
I too had felt the toil and heat,
The wind and storm I did not fear.

Perhaps the Heavenward look in store,
The speechless prayer for strength or rest,
Might help those needy spirits more
Than hope set forth, or joy expressed.
But I was changed, I knew not how,
By the same love that chose their ways, --
I might be just as weary now,
And yet rejoice to hear Thy praise.

Now would I cheer the faint in heart
With sound of joy they too shall see;
Now would I put the fear apart,
That bids me hide Thy strength in me.
What though the mortal flesh be frail,
The willing spirit prone to sink --
There is a stream in Baca's vale,
Whereof Thy feeblest child may drink.

Some, in their sorrow, may not know
How near their feet those waters glide --
How peaceful fruits for healing grow,
And flowers for beauty by their side.
They may not see, with weeping eyes
Upon the dreary desert bent,
How glorious straight before them, lies
The Eden of their soul's content.

But, O my Savior, I can see
For them, what once for me was seen;
I know, whate'er their sufferings be,
The tender mercy which they mean.
I do not watch, with anxious care,
To see the end of their distress --
Thou knowest what the heart must bear,
The human heart which Thou wilt bless.

And in their daily deepening need
Of heavenly love, for strength or rest,
They are already blest indeed --
Yea, and much more they shall be blest.
Wrapt in the spirit of Thy praise,
As from Gerizim's height, I see
Blessing poured out on all the ways,
That prove Thy children's need of Thee.

O wondrous love, so strong to smite --
So meek the opposing will to tame!
It was Thy hand put forth in might,
That led me through the flood, the flame.
When, needing strength to bear Thy rod,
By the smooth stream I found repose,
It was Thy grace, All-seeing God,
Thy love that smote me, ere I rose.

How could I look for lengthened rest,
With Thy deep sufferings scarcely known,
Or lay forever on Thy breast,
The perfect heart which Thou wilt own?
The heart, that guilty of Thy woes,

Looks only upon Thee to mourm,
And feels the cross Thy love bestows,
A burden easy to be borne.

And yet that pause was not in vain --
It was a blessing meet to give
Strength, for the labor and the pain,
Whereby alone my soul might live.
How gently thence Thy mighty hand
My lingering spirit onward bare!
How precious, in a barren land,
The footprints of Thy people were!

There many hearts that knew Thy ways
The safety of my soul could see --
And there I heard the song of praise,
That Faith poured out to Heaven for me.
O, more than all the ease I sought,
That song the desert path could bless
And dearer in my deepest thought,
The love that met me in distress.

Now that Thy mercies on my head
The oil of joy for mourning pour, --
Not as I will my steps be led,
But as Thou wilt for evermore.
Henceforth, whate'er my heart's desire,
Fulfil in me Thy own design,
I need the fountain and the fire --
And both, O King of Saints, are thine.

Now that my sense of rest in Thee,
Rules over every rising fear,
Pain, pleasure, all I feel and see,
Thy counsels to my soul endear.
Now can my girded heart rejoice,
In praise poured out, in love expressed --
Now may I bless Thee, with a voice
That shall not break this sacred rest.

HYMN 18

NATURAL AFFECTION IN THE NEW CREATURE

"It is sown a natural body; it is raised a spiritual body." -- I Cor. 15:44.

Jesus, Lord of Heaven above,
Earth beneath is all Thy own
In the depths of Heavenly love
Let my human heart be sown.

Let my love that as a grain
None on earth might care to see,
Buried in Thy grave remain,
Be a precious seed to Thee.

Thou wilt raise it, though it die,
Thou wilt see it hidden there --
Thou wilt guard it with Thine eye
From the spirits of the air.

None shall take it thence away;
It is sown for Thy delight:
Thou wilt shine on it by day, --
Thou wilt shield it in the night.

Where the silent waters flow,
It shall multiply its root;
It shall blossom, it shall grow,
It shall bear immortal fruit.

Sown in weakness, raised in power --
Sown in suffering, raised in peace --
It shall brave the blighting hour,
In the year of drought increase.

Never hurt by sun or storm,
Blest its every stage shall be;
Dying in its mortal form --
Living evermore in Thee.

HYMN 19

"Thou wilt keep him in perfect peace, whose mind is stayed in Thee: because he trusteth in Thee." -- Isaiah 26:3.

O, this is blessing, this is rest --
Unto Thine arms, O Lord, I flee:
I hide me in Thy faithful breast,
And pour out all my soul to Thee.
There is a host dissuading me, --
But, all their voices far above,
I hear Thy words -- "O taste and see
The comfort of a Savior's love."
And, hushing every adverse sound,
Songs of defence my soul surround,
As if all saints encamped about
One trusting heart pursued by doubt,

And O, how solemn, yet how sweet
Their one assured, persuasive strain!
"The Lord of hosts is thy retreat,
The Man who bore thy sin, thy pain.
Still in His hand thy times remain --
Still of his body thou art part;
And He will prove his right to reign
O'er all things that concern thy heart."
O tenderness -- O truth divine!
Lord, I am altogether thine.
I have bowed down -- I need not flee --
Peace, peace is mine in trusting Thee.

And now I count supremely kind,
The rule that once I thought severe;
And, precious to my altered mind,
At length, Thy least reproofs appear.
Now to the love that casts out fear,
Mercy and truth, indeed seem one;
Why should I hold my ease so dear?
The work of training must be done,
I must be taught what I would know --
I must be led where I would go --
And all the rest ordained for me,
Till that which is not seen I see
Is to be found in trusting Thee.

HYMN 20

"The Lord is my portion, saith my soul; therefore will I hope in Him."
-- Lam. 3:24.

My heart is resting, O my God, --
I will give thanks and sing;
My heart is at the secret source
Of every precious thing.
Now the frail vessel Thou hast made
No hand but Thine shall fill --
For the waters of the Earth have failed,
And I am thirsty still.

I thirst for springs of heavenly life,
And here all day they rise --
I seek the treasure of Thy love,
And close at hand it lies.
And a new song is in my mouth
To long loved music set --
Glory to Thee for all the grace
I have not tasted yet.

Glory to Thee for strength withheld,
For want and weakness known --
And the fear that sends me to Thy breast
For what is most my own.
I have a heritage of joy
That yet I must not see;
But the hand that bled to make it mine
Is keeping it for me.

There is a certainty of love
That sets my heart at rest --
A calm assurance for today
That to be poor is best --
A prayer reposing on His truth
Who hath made all things mine,
That draws my captive will to Him,
And makes it one with Thine.

I will give thanks for suffering now,
For want and toil and loss --
For the death that sin makes hard and slow,
Upon my Savior's cross --

Thanks for the little spring of love
That gives me strength to say,
If they will leave me part in Him,
Let all things pass away.

Sometimes I long for promised bliss,
But it will not come too late --
And the songs of patient spirits rise
From the place wherein I wait;
While in the faith that makes no haste
My soul has time to see
A kneeling host of Thy redeemed,
In fellowship with me.

There is a multitude around
Responsive to my prayer;
I hear the voice of my desire
Resounding everywhere.
But the earnest of eternal joy,
In every prayer I trace;
I see the glory of the Lord:
On every chastened face.

How oft, in still communion known,
Those spirits have been sent
To share the travail of my soul,
Or show me what it meant!
And I long to do some work of love
No spoiling hand could touch,
For the poor and suffering of Thy flock
Who comfort me so much.

But the yearning thought is mingled now
With the thankful song I sing;
For Thy people know the secret source
Of every precious thing.
The heart that ministers for Thee
In Thy own work will rest;
And the subject spirit of a child
Can serve Thy children best.

Mine be the reverent, listening love,
That waits all day on Thee,
With the service of a watchful heart
Which no one else can see --
The faith that, in a hidden way
No other eye may know,
Finds all its daily work prepared,
And loves to have it so.

My heart is resting, O my God,
My heart is in Thy care --
I hear the voice of joy and health
Resounding everywhere.
"Thou art my portion," saith my soul,
Ten thousand voices say,
And the music of their glad Amen,
Will never die away.

HYMN 21

"I will allure her, and bring her into the wilderness, and speak comfortably unto her. And I will give her her vineyards from thence, and the valley of Achor for a door of hope; and she shall sing there." -- Hosea 2:14,15.

"I know, O Lord, that Thy judgments are right, and that Thou in faithfulness hast afflicted me." -- Psalm 119:75.

I will love Thee, O Lord, my strength --
Thee shall my rescued heart embrace;
Thy love, in all its breadth and length,
Shall be my peaceful dwelling place.
Whom have I on the earth beside?
Thy cross, Thy crown of thorns I see;
Thou who to save my life hast died,
I will have fellowship with Thee.

Surely Thy human heart has borne
My greatest grief, my least distress --
Surely I see my Savior mourn
With the bowed spirit He will bless
Nailed to Thy cross, I would not fly
The pain it grieves Thy soul to give:
If because Thou hast died I die,
Because Thou livest I shall live.

How could a moment's pang destroy
My heart's confirmed repose in Thee?
Thy presence is sufficient joy
To one reclaimed and spared like me.
It is enough that I am Thine --
Almighty to redeem from sin;
Thou shalt subdue, correct, refine
The heart which Thou hast died to win.

Now, through this light and passing pain,
The travail of Thy soul I see --
I know Thou hast not borne in vain
The mortal anguish due to me;
Thoughts of a love unfelt before
In comfort on my heart descend --
This suffering must have cost Thee more
Than I can ever comprehend.

Yet, through a sacred sympathy,
I of Thy precious death partake
I feel my fellowship with Thee,
And with the Father for Thy sake.
I see the source of all Thy woe,
Thy resurrection's power I feel --
And streams of living waters flow
Through the dry desert where I kneel.

Shielded from every fear of wrath, --
Looking through love on all that is --
I see about my troubled path
A cloud of tranquil witnesses.
Happy the chastening to endure,
That makes me one, in love and trust,
With all the lowly, all the pure,
All the tried spirits of the just.

Thy children's sympathy is sweet,
But all is measured -- all in part;
Into Thy love my hopes retreat,
For that which satisfles the heart.
There may be other love in store,
But none whereof Thy child may say --
My strength, my life, for evermore,
My ample portion day by day.

Such solace as around me grows,
Thou for my need shalt still prepare --
But make Thy bosom my repose,
And fix my expectation there.
For Thou canst cherish and uphold
Life, that no eye but Thine may see --
And no rough wind, no heat, or cold,
Shall hurt the love that clings to Thee.

In to Thy silent place of prayer,
The anxious, wandering mind recall --
Dwell mid Thy own creation there,
Restoring, claiming, hallowing all.
Then the calm spirit, won from sin,
Thy perfect sacrifice shall be --
And all the ransomed powers therein
Shall go forth, glorifying Thee.

Out of this spirit of Thy grace,
O, who can tell what light has beamed!
I see the solitary place,
A garden for Thy own redeemed.
I see the desolated ground,

With dews of Heavenly kindness fed --
And fruits of joy and love surround
The heart which Thou hast comforted.

O knowledge all my thoughts above!
This thirsty vale I could not flee,
This yearning for unbounded love
Has been "a door of hope" to me.
Who would go forth in haste by flight,
From the dry land which Thou wilt bless --
Sown with the everlasting light,
That shows Thy "very faithfulness!"

Thou hast loved me, O Lord, my strength;
On Thee my yielded heart shall lean;
Thy guiding love in all its length
Shall teach me all Thy judgments mean.
And I will ask Thee for a sign
That many an anxious eye may see --
Give me the love that rests in Thine,
For those whom Thou hast tried like me.

Love that believes, is always sweet
To fearful hearts, which Thou wilt guide,
And mine may win some timid feet,
To the deep River's quiet side.
While from that River's fertile banks,
My resting eye their portion sees --
O that my, soul might yield Thee thanks;
By comforting the least of these.

HYMN 22

"Deep calleth unto deep at the noise of Thy waterspouts; all Thy waves and Thy billows are gone over me. Yet the Lord will command His lovingkindness in the daytime, and in the night his song shall be with me, and my prayer unto the God of my life." -- Psalm 42:7,8.

Be not far from me, O my strength,
Whom all my times obey;
Take from me anything Thou wilt;
But go not Thou away, --
And let the storm that does Thy work
Deal with me as it may.

On Thy compassion I repose,
In weakness and distress:
I will not ask for greater ease,
Lest I should love Thee less.
O, 'tis a blessed thing for me
To need Thy tenderness.

While many sympathizing hearts
For my deliverance care,
Thou, in Thy wiser, stronger love,
Art teaching me to bear --
By the sweet voice of thankful song,
And calm, confiding prayer.

Thy love has many a lighted path,
No outward eye can trace,
And my heart sees Thee in the deep,
With darkness on its face,
And communes with Thee, mid the storm,
As in a secret place.

O comforter of God's redeemed,
Whom the world does not see,
What hand should pluck me from the flood,
That casts my soul on Thee?
Who would not suffer pain like mine,
To be consoled like me?

When I am feeble as a child,
And flesh and heart give way,
Then on Thy everlasting strength,

With passive trust I stay,
And the rough wind becomes a song,
The darkness shines like day.

O, blessed are the eyes that see,
Though silent anguish show,
The love that in their hours of sleep,
Unthanked may come and go.
And blessed are the ears that hear,
Though kept awake by woe.

Happy are they that learn, in Thee,
Though patient suffering teach,
The secret of enduring strength,
And praise too deep for speech --
Peace that no pressure from without,
No strife within can reach.

There is no death for me to fear,
For Christ, my Lord, hath died;
There is no curse in this my pain,
For he was crucified.
And it is fellowship with Him
That keeps me near His side.

My heart is fixed, O God, my strength --
My heart is strong to bear;
I will be joyful in Thy love;
And peaceful in Thy care.
Deal with me, for my Savior's sake,
According to His prayer.

No suffering while it lasts is joy,
How blest soe'er it be --
Yet may the chastened child be glad
His Father's face to see
And O, it is not hard to bear,
What must be borne in Thee.

It is not hard to bear by faith,
In Thy own bosom laid,
The trial of a soul redeemed,
For Thy rejoicing made.
Well may the heart in patience rest,
That none can make afraid.

Safe in Thy sanctifying grace,
Almighty to restore --
Borne onward -- sin and death behind,
And love and life before --

O, let my soul abound in hope,
And praise Thee more and more!

Deep unto deep may call, but I
With peaceful heart will say --
Thy loving-kindness hath a charge
No waves can take away;
And let the storm that speeds me home,
Deal with me as it may.

HYMN 23

"God is faithful, by whom ye were called unto the fellowship of his Son Jesus Christ our Lord." -- 1 Cor. 1:6.

Bowed with a burden none can weigh save Thee,
Strength of my life, on Thee I cast my care;
My heart must prove its own infirmity,
But what shall move me, if my God be there?

O for a thankful song with every breath,
While amid fading flowers and withering grass,
I, with Thee, through the grave and gate of death,
On to my joyful resurrection pass.

Armed with the spirit of my Master's mind,
How shall I spare a thought that He would slay?
Lord I would leave those things which are behind,
And press towards Heaven through all the narrow way.

Bright be my prospect as I pass along; --
An ardent service at the cost of all, --
Love by untiring ministry made strong,
And ready for the first, the softest call.

Yes, God is faithful -- and my lot is cast;
O not myself to serve, my own to be!
Light of my life, the darkness now is past,
And I beneath the Cross can work for Thee.

HYMN 24

"He that loveth his life shall lose it: and he that hateth his life in this world shall keep it unto life eternal." -- John 12:25.

Sweet be Thy words of sternest truth,
My risen Lord to me!
Hid in the secret of my heart
Their deepest treasure be;
That I may comprehend the joy
Of sacrifice for Thee.

And, softly let the light of life,
Before Thy servant shine,
That through the gloom with steadfast will,
My soul may follow Thine --
Calm in the depth of one desire,
And strong in one design.

But never let me think I see
Thy heavenly things aright,
Unless the single eye of love
Fill my whole mind with light,
And to be like Thee in Thy death
Seems glorious in my sight.

That willing sacrifice of Thine
My meditation make,
Till to the true delight of life
My soul with songs awake, --
And all that spoils me of myself
Be treasure for Thy sake.

The tenderest heart Thy hands have made
Beneath Thy rule may rest;
For He who made it for Himself
Knows what will shield it best, --
The feeblest lover of Thy law,
Dwells safely in Thy breast.

Now through, a strait and painful way
My weary feet must press;
But what shall hurt the struggling soul
Which Thou hast died to bless,
Or prompt a spirit to complain

That knows its blessedness!

Nor seems it strange to one who weighs
The joy of liberty,
This death of suffering to himself,
This life of love to Thee,
Which gives the lowly power to reign
And makes the servant free.

O let no timid faithless thought
Prevail my bonds to spare!
Lord, I can drink Thy bitter cup,
Thy fiery trial share, --
I can deny myself for Thee,
And for Thy glory care.

Only the unction of Thy love,
With every cross be mine --
Till these Thy words -- so firm to gird,
So searching to refine --
Be sweet unto Thy servant's soul
Even as they are to Thine.

HYMN 25

*"It is a faithful saying: For if we be dead with Him, we shall also live with Him:
if we suffer, we shall also reign with Him." -- 2 Tim 2:11,12.*

*"Most gladly therefore will I rather glory in my infirmities, that the power of
Christ may rest upon me." -- 2 Cor. 12:9.*

Compassed about with songs, my soul was still --
But not for lack of light its bliss to see;
Thy heart, my Father, could the temple fill,
And its deep silence was a song to Thee.
My mind reposed in its captivity,
By the clear evidence of love subdued;
I was content to die, that I might be
Redeemed forever from my solitude.
All that was in me to Thy throne aspired
Longed for Thy heavenly glory to be meet, --
Devotion was the joy to be desired,
And the the thought of sacrifice was sweet.

But He who knew my frame was training me
For service needing strength that cannot wane,
And teaching me my frail mortality
By solemn reckonings of the weight of pain.
I in my weakness -- how was I to reign,
When suffering was the only way to power?
And would my spirit in His strength remain,
When watching was a strife for one short hour?
Conid I with steadfast heart myself deny?
Could I with patient love the Cross endure?
Should I be every day content to die,
To keep my daily life in Him secure?

Then with fresh sweetness, from the saints in light,
One song of victory to my soul made known,
How the hid treasure of the Church's might
Was in the power of her Beloved alone.
And then Thy glory to my heart was shown,
Even as the glory of the blest above; --
I knew Thy steadfast spirit was my own,
By the pure joy of Thy reflected love.

Miss A. L. Waring

And the mind communed with me that was his
Who said "When I am weak then am I strong" --
Until the voice of my infirmities
Made harmony with that triumphant song.

HYMN 26

"Arise, walk through the land in the length of it and in the breadth of it; for I will give it unto thee." -- Gen. 13:7.

"All things are yours ... things present." -- 1 Cor. 3:21,22.

While toil and warfare urge us on our way,
And heart is answering heart in signs of pain,
Have we no words of strengthening joy to say --
No songs for those who suffer but to reign?

O for the faithful mind, the steadfast eye,
To keep our Leader's glory full in sight,
And make our converse, even while we die,
An interchange of triumph and delight.

Behold, the paths of life are ours -- we see
Our blest inheritance where'er we tread;
Sorrow and danger our security,
And disappointment lifting up our head.

Kings unto God, we may not doubt our power,
We may not languish when He says, "Be strong" --
We must move on through every adverse hour,
And take possession as we pass along.

Yes, all is for us -- nothing shall withstand
Our faithful, valiant, persevering claim; --
The rod of God's Anointed in our hand,
And our assurance His unchanging name.

We need no haste where He, has said "Be still" --
No peace where He has charged us to contend;
Only the fearless love to do His will,
And to show forth His honor to the end.

O ye that faint and die, arise and live!
Sing, ye that all things have a charge to bless!
If He is faithful who hath sworn to give,
Then be ye also faithful, and possess.

Take thy whole portion with thy Master's mind --
Toil, hindrance, hardness, with His virtue take --
And think how short a time thy heart may find

To labor or to suffer for His sake.

Count all the pains that speed thee to thy rest
Among the riches of thy purchased right,
Yea, bind them in His name upon thy breast,
As jewels for the Bride, the Lamb's delight.

And love shall teach us while on Him we lean,
That, in the certainty of coming bliss,
We may be yearning for a world unseen,
Yet wear our beautiful array in this.

Ours be a loyal love for service tried,
To show, by deeds and words and looks that cheer,
How He can bless the scene in which He died,
And fill His house with glory even here.

HYMN 27

"Jesus said unto His disciples, If any man will come after me, let him deny himself; and take up his cross, and follow me." -- Matt 16:24.

"I lead in the way of righteousness, in the midst of the paths of judgment, that I may cause those that love me to inherit substance, and I will fill their treasures." -- Prov. 8:20,21.

Heavenly things my soul hath seen,
Things the Holy Spirit shows, --
Things on which the heart can lean
When the flesh has no repose.
All was light, and life and rest --
Love was mine, and I was blest:
Every pain I had to bear
Proved my Shepherd's tender care;
Everything I had to do
Taught my heart that He was true:
I could choose the way He trod,
I could give my will to God.
Waters still and pastures green,
Pleasant paths my soul hath seen.

Is it all a vision gone!
Was the gladness all in vain?
Oh to travel firmly on!
Oh to tread those paths again!
Lord, on Thee my help is laid;
Thou art true, but I have strayed; --
Left Thee with a froward will,
Strayed from One who loves me still.
Through the tangled waste I see,
Seek the sheep that pants for Thee.
Show me the forsaken track,
Lead Thy wanderer safely back:
Let no fear my steps withhold
From the flock within Thy fold.

Sacred memories do not cease --
Still my heart, where'er I go,
Sees the river of thy peace
Through those pleasant pastures flow,
Still, amid the desert drear,
Songs of heavenly love I hear.

Heavenly love! the sound is sweet,
Lo, it stays my wandering feet, --
Leads to Thee for all I lack, --
Softly bids me welcome back.
Thoughts of perfect gifts it brings,
Thoughts of deep enduring things, --
Thoughts of joy I yet may see
Hidden in Thy word for me.

O my Savior! never more
From my treasure to depart,
Now my failing will restore,
Fix the purpose of my heart.
Let Thy spirit in me be
Springing up in love to Thee.
Listening, following day by day,
Steadfast in my onward way,
Girded with Thy faithful mind,
Pleasant paths I yet shall find.
Fonntains at my feet shall rise,
Riches hid shall meet mine eyes.

Songs of glory to my God
In the desert shall be heard!
There is comfort in Thy rod,
Power in Thy reproving word.
In a spirit all thine own
Make Thy hardest sayings known.
They will guard me with Thy strength,
Bear me all my journey's length;
Give me for the daily strife,
Joy and health and plenteous life.
Hid within for precious fruit,
Love shalt take eternal root --
Love that in the Spirit lives;
Love that grows by all it gives.
Neath a rule so firm to bless,
I shall learn Thy gentleness.
Show it forth in all I do,
Making others feel it too.

Savior! fast the moments flee --
O decide my will today.
Bind my heart to follow Thee
Ere the song has died away.
Never let a fear or pain
Turn me to myself again.
Though my strength has failed me long,
Let Thy promise make me strong --
Strong my nature to withstand, --

Strong to hold Thy guiding hand.
All the joy before me set
Teach me never to forget.
If indeed with Thee to stay
I must choose a narrow way, --
If my inmost heart must give
All its purpose, thus to live, --
Still, my portion Thou must be,
Still my spirit cries to Thee.
O for all Thy light to shine!
O for love to keep me Thine.

HYMN 28

"I commune with mine own heart." -- Psalm 77:6.

Ere another step I take
In my wilful wandering way,
Still I have a choice to make --
Shall I alter while I may?

Patient love is waiting still
In my Savior's heart for me;
Love to bend my froward will,
Love to make me really free.

Far from Him, what can I gain?
Want and shame, and bondage vile --
Better far to bear the pain
Of His yoke a little while.

Soon I might its comfort find;
Soon my thankful heart might cry,
"In Thy meek obedient mind,
As Thou walkest so would I."

In His paths what could I lack?
God's own hand my cup would fill;
Hark! my Savior calls me back --
Shall I turn with all my will?

Still His wisdom I may get --
Learn to labor while I pray.
Striving till my feet be set
Firmly in the narrow way.

HYMN 29

A RESURRECTION HYMN.
"The Lord is risen."

Dear Savior of a dying world,
Where grief and change must be,
In the new grave where Thou wast laid
My heart lies down with Thee.
O, not in cold despair of joy,
Or weariness of pain,
But from a hope that shall not die,
To rise and live again.

I would arise in all Thy strength
My place on earth to fill,
To work out all my time of war
With love's unflinchng will.
Firm against every doubt of Thee
For all my future way --
To walk in Heaven's eternal light
Throughout the changing day.

Ah, such a day as Thou shalt own
When suns have ceased to shine
A day of burdens borne by Thee,
And work that all was Thine.
Speed Thy bright rising in my heart,
Thy righteous kingdom speed, --
Till my whole life in concord say,
"The Lord is risen indeed."

O for an impulse from Thy love
With every coming breath,
To sing that sweet undying song
Amid the wrecks of death!
A "hail!" to every mortal pang
That bids me take my right
To glory in the blessed life
Which Thou hast brought to light.

I long to see the hallowed earth
In new creation rise,
To find the germs of Eden hid
Where its fallen beauty lies, --

To feel the spring-tide of a soul
By one deep love set free,
Made meet to lay aside her dust
And be at home with Thee.

And then -- there shall be yet an end --
An end now full to bless!
How dear to those who watch for Thee
With human tenderness.
Then shall the saying come to pass
That makes our hope complete,
And, rising from the conquered grave,
Thy parted ones shall meet.

Yes -- they shall meet, and face to face
By heart to heart be known,
Clothed with Thy Likeness, Lord of Life,
And perfect in their own.
For this corruptible must rise
From its corruption free,
And this frail mortal must put on
Thine immortality.

Shine then, Thou Resurrection Light,
Upon our sorrows shine!
The fulness of Thy joy be ours,
As all our griefs were Thine.
Now in this changing, dying life
Our faded hopes restore,
Till, in Thy triumph perfected,
We taste of death no more.

HYMN 30

A NEW-YEAR HYMN.

Sunlight of the heavenly day,
Mighty to revive and cheer,
Bless our yet untrodden way,
Lead us through the entered year.
Where the shades of death we see,
Let Thy living brightness be --
Let it speed our lingering feet --
Let it shine on all we meet.
While before our chastened gaze
Earthly pleasures fade and fail,
Thou, the light of all our days --
Thou, our steadfast glory, hail!

Forward, though the path be hid;
Though we pass the lurking foe;
Though the sound of war forbid,
Girt with gladness, let its go.
Bold in Thy protecting care,
Strong to prove Thee faithful there
Through the desert or the sea,
On, to reign in life with Thee.
Ah, with more than fearless heart,
Homeward be our faces set;
Show us in our present part
Wealth we have not measured yet.

Open Thou beneath our tread
Springs the distance could not show;
From the holy Fountain-head,
Let them rise where'er we go.
Rather give us eyes to see --
Love awake to love in Thee --
Hearts that, trusting in Thy care,
Find its traces everywhere.
Teach us, as we pass along,
In the shining of Thy face,
Many a sweet thanksgiving-song,
Even in a dreary place.

While with firm, unyielding will
For the victor's crown we strive,

Gracious Savior, keep us still
To Thy gentlest signs alive --
Where the stormy wind is heard,
Quick to every tender word,
And for all our journey's length,
Armed with meekness more than strength.
In the shadow of Thy hand
We can brave the uprooting gale,
And a little child may stand
Where the soldier's heart would fail.

Oft a desolating blast
Bears the seed of comfort too,
And the patient soul at last
Finds a garden where it blew;
So, where nothing cheers our sight,
Germs of love may spring to light,
Bright 'mid earth's oppressive shades,
Fresh beside the leaf that fades.
Let the precious seed abound --
Make the tempest strong to bless,
Strong to claim our thorny ground
For the fruits of holiness.

Lord of All! we cannot know
What our paths may yet unfold;
But the part that love would show --
Wise to save us -- Thou hast told.
By our heart's unmeasured price --
By Thy life-long sacrifice --
By Thy death to set us free,
Lead us on to joy in Thee.
On, to greet the perfect day,
Blessed End of time and strife, --
On, through all the shinlng way,
Brightness of our human life.

HYMN 31

BEREAVEMENT.

Flow on, Thou Fountain of my joy,
Through all the wilderness!
Thou seest what will work for good,
Thou knowest how to bless.
Get Thyself glory, O my God,
Be praised in my distress!

O, let Thy true, refining love
Its utmost pleasure see
And lift not up Thy faithful hand
Whate'er my cry may be,
Till I am strong for Thy renown,
And pure for use to Thee.

I know Thine eye has weighed the path
To Thy lost creature's bliss.
No comfort could supply the need
Of grief so sore as this; --
No joy could wake my heart so well
To Thy full preciousness.

Thou wast the Source of all that love
Which makes me glad no more, --
And Thou hast taken to Thyself
What was Thine own before.
Thine, and mine too, O Good to give,
O Faithful to restore.

That loving spirit is withdrawn
From every shade of sin;
And I in sympathy with her
A holier life begin.
Yes! to her new delight in Thee,
I, Lord, can enter in.

She with Thee, wheresoe'er Thou art,
In fellowship untold!
She in Thee, living by my Bread,
My hope, my heart's stronghold!
O! 'tis a song for days of grief,
Whate'er their depths unfold.

As one whose mother comforts him,
I will lift up my head.
No wound of Thine shall take the life
From words which Thou hast said,
And in the fulness of Thy truth
I shall be comforted.

HYMN 32

"Whosoever will lose his life for my sake shall find it." -- Matt. 16:25.

O! there is more than ear hath heard,
Light of the World, in this Thy word!
It speaks the living soul to win;
It claims the loving heart within;
It tells us inly understood,
That Thou art God, that Thou art good.
Here our fallen nature raised we see, --
Here our lost glory shines in Thee, --
And man sees man in mortal strife,
A witness that to love is life.

Yes, for Thy sake -- O strong to bear!
The secret of Thy strength was there.
'Twas not the power which gave us breath,
That urged Thee through the gates of death,
That bade Thee tread the press alone
To make the Father's message known.
It was Thy spirit's deep intent
It was Thy love for Him who sent;
It was His joy that bore Thee through,
And he who sees Thee sees Him too.

Yes, for Thy sake, O God Most High,
O! Man Most Meek, we too can die: --
Die to the death which Thou hast slain,
Die to the deepest source of pain,
And walk, by Love's sustaining store,
As seekers of our own no more.

We can hear more than ear hath heard,
Life of the World! in this Thy word;
And wastes shall break forth into song,
As in its power we pass along.

For lo! in hidden deep accord,
The servant may be like his Lord.
And Thy love our love shining through,
May tell the world that Thou art true,
Till those who see us see Thee too.